The Release

Also by Jeremy Hooker

FROM SHEARSMAN BOOKS

Upstate: A North American Journal
Openings: A European Journal
Diary of a Stroke
Ancestral Lines
Word and Stone
The Art of Seeing
Selected Poems 1965–2018

FROM OTHER PUBLISHERS

POETRY
Landscape of the Daylight Moon
Soliloquies of a Chalk Giant
Solent Shore
Englishman's Road
A View from the Source
Master of the Leaping Figures
Their Silence a Language (with Lee Grandjean)
Our Lady of Europe
Adamah
Arnolds Wood
The Cut of the Light: Poems 1965–2005
Scattered Light
Under the Quarry Wood

PROSE
Welsh Journal

CRITICISM
Poetry of Place
The Presence of the Past: Essays on Modern British and American Poetry
Writers in a Landscape
Imagining Wales: A View of Modern Welsh Writing in English
Ditch Vision

AS EDITOR:
Frances Bellerby: *Selected Stories*
Alun Lewis: *Selected Poems* (with Gweno Lewis)
At Home on Earth: A New Selection of the Later Writings of Richard Jefferies
Alun Lewis: *Inwards Where All the Battle Is: Writings from India*
Mapping Golgotha: A Selection of Wilfred Owen's Letters and Poems
Edward Thomas: *The Ship of Swallows*

Jeremy Hooker

The Release

Shearsman Books

First published in the United Kingdom in 2022 by
Shearsman Books Ltd
PO Box 4239
Swindon
SN3 9FN

Shearsman Books Ltd Registered Office
30–31 St. James Place, Mangotsfield, Bristol BS16 9JB
(this address not for correspondence)

www.shearsman.com

ISBN 978-1-84861-799-5

ACKNOWLEDGEMENTS
My thanks are due to the editors of the following journals
in which some of these poems have appeared:
Agenda, Poetry Wales, Red Poets, Scintilla, Shearsman magazine.

I owe a special debt of gratitude to Christopher Meredith and
Philip Gross for their close, critical reading of some of the poems,
which helped me to revise them.

Contents

Foreword   9

1.

Diary 19/20 June – 10 July 2019   11

2.

Diary 29 August – 27 September 2019   32

3. *Poems*

Night in June   42
Under observation   43
Old men in ward 7   44
Elwin   45
Clouds at evening   46
Wanting sleep   47
 Solstice   48
View from ward 7   49
In and out of the ward   50
Escape   51
Kuzula   52
Baby and mother   53
Symphony   54
Antithesis   55
Conversation   56
Seagull   57
Constable cloud study   58
Home   59

4.

Diary 26 April – 28 May 2020   60

5. *Poems*

Widower   73
On a painting by David Jones   74
In praise of windows   75
A philosopher in search of the soul   76

6.

Diary 9 July – 7 August 2020   79

7. *Poems*

Nurses   88
The Bridge   89
White Horse Hill   90
Homage to the author of Flowering Earth   91
Gulls   93
Archie   94
A Squib for Archie   95

For the nurses and doctors of
Prince Charles Hospital, Merthyr Tydfil
and of the Renal Unit at The Heath in Cardiff

Foreword

Since *Welsh Journal* (2001), I have periodically adopted a form of writing that juxtaposes prose and poetry. *The Release* is a work of this kind, in which diary entries and poems are combined and interact. Roughly speaking, the diary records experience that generates the poems, or, to use another metaphor, the poems disclose their roots in the prose.

Between June 2019 and August 2020, I spent four long periods in hospital, initially in Prince Charles Hospital in Merthyr Tydfil, and latterly in the Renal Unit at The Heath in Cardiff. The diary records my experience as a patient and reflects aspects of the life of the hospital; the poems respond to what I felt and saw in the ward, but also go beyond being a record of everyday reality. Like my *Diary of a Stroke* and other journals, *The Release* is a poet's journal. In ways that the book describes, the periods of hospitalization proved to be intensely creative. This was partly due to having so much time to write and read and think, together with the ever-present sense of mortality. Long days and some sleepless nights in bed were conducive to memory, and stimulated me to write, as well as the poems, rough drafts of two books: *Addiction: a love story*, and a memoir of my life in Wales. These are, as it were, backgrounds to the material of which *The Release* is composed.

In editing the material, I have focused mainly on two things: the reality of days and nights confined to a hospital bed, and the life of the mind, intellectual and spiritual, which finds expression in poetry. At times, in the process of writing poems, or drafts of poems, I was acutely aware of the workings of the imagination, and of feeling my way to a better understanding of poetry as a magnetic 'field of force'. As I wrote in the diary, I realized that: 'A stream of thinking and feeling, a lyrical stream, has been released in my mind'. This is partly what *The Release* is about, and I have edited the diary with this theme in mind. But this is not only a book concerned with poetry, or with self-reflection. It is also a tribute to the modern hospital as a place of care and healing. In Prince Charles Hospital and at The Heath, I experienced 'the reality of democracy' that characterises our National Health Service. This was all the more impressive in contrast to the noise of the outer, political world, and in view of the pressures on staff due to the Covid virus.

1.

Unable to get out of bed this morning, and after a night when I thought I might die, two young ambulance women arrived to bump me down the stairs, hazardously, on a stretcher and take me into hospital, where I was placed in an observation room. I was alert enough to know we were going to Prince Charles Hospital in Merthyr, and not the hospital in which Mieke died. Initial opinion seems to be that I have an infection due to under functioning kidneys. Coincidentally, after at first being too weak to take any interest in my post, I opened a packet from Shearsman to find the first copy of *Word and Stone* inside.

Summer Solstice

Of course, I've read my new book over & over. Several doctors & nurses have been impressed by having a poet under observation. More importantly, I've laid in bed working on what may become a long poem. I had started reading Robert Duncan's *The H.D. Book* before coming into hospital. Duncan's treatment of images (and The Image) impressed me very much. Thereafter, I began to lose patience. There's something about Duncan's treatment of the imagination, and virtual deification of poetry, that makes me feel queasy. I know Duncan was a true poet, probably a great one, but for me his myth of Reality is ultimately vacuous, unlike David Jones'.

I've never been happy with the idea of Poetry as a religion – religions may be poetic, and sources of great poetry, but Poetry tends to gather awe to itself, instead of being in awe of what is beyond it – Being, Reality, God, however understood. Pride in our minds leads to a kind of soft-headed egotism. We must never lose sight of what is beyond us, and what has made us, instead of exalting our own makings.

Evening of the longest day. From the window I can see a line of cloud along the hill outside Merthyr, houses, and two wind turbines, arms moving. Unable to walk, I especially observe movements – traffic, small figures walking, turbines. Meanwhile, I'm missing news of the great

Brexit circus, and the clown show that threatens to impose Boris Johnson on us as our 'Leader'. What a dangerous farce. How has Democracy failed as to put the world in the hands of men such as Trump & Johnson?

Trump and his mindless acolytes make big noises about making America GREAT again. Greatness is the last thing we need. Humility and common sense would be wonderful. And how many would vote for that?

Two squibs, written to cheer myself up and for the amusement of friends.

Wise Words

'What matters,' she said,
is not how long we live,
but how well.'

Which was fine in a woman of 97
who'd once burst naked
out of a birthday cake
at a party of business suits.

And fallen on her feet,
and married an archduke,
and after, one by one
(for she was no bigamist)
three earls, all dying young
of exhaustion, at the peak of wealth.

GREAT

WE ARE GREAT
proclaims a mighty voice,
a trumpet blast
                    that shakes the globe.

FORGET the masses huddled
on the grimy streets
the unschooled children
and the sick without a dollar
or a friend
FORGET the lesser breeds
       beyond the wall.

DON'T THINK of them:
the white bear floating
on a warming sea,
the albatross
entangled in the plastic tide.

FOR WE ARE GREAT
and will be **GREATER** yet

FORGET this piece of dirt
this particle, this blue spot
floating in a waste of space
as we look down

This is the voyage of your lives, my friends.
So, beam me up
and on our spacecraft
probing gaps between the stars
inscribe in words of steel
your **GREATNESS** & **MY NAME**

Sunday 23 June

I have rather lost a sense of time since being brought into hospital. I'd become hazy about time when unwell at home. Just now, after breakfast, a team of physiotherapists got me into a chair and helped me to wash. They'll come again later to help me to walk a little. 20 years ago, my stroke was a wake-up call that I answered only intermittently. Lying in bed, or sitting in this chair, I feel quite well in myself, but the disease has made me literally legless, and I haven't touched a drop of strong drink! After immersion in *The H.D. Book* it's a relief to turn back to Barry Lopez's *Horizon*. Lopez's focus on real things – people, places, history, ideas – reminds me of my excitement, years ago, at reading J. M. Synge's book about the Aran Islands. Realism should be a starting point, not a terminus. Instead of an end in itself, it should be a stimulus for imagination, for going beyond.

Afternoon

Began writing *Addiction: A Love Story*

Earlier, I walked a little, supported by Lauren (physio) & a zimmer. I remembered a similar experience following my stroke, and M. telling me that when she saw me walking with the zimmer, I had looked such an old man, she had wept. Now, I felt her absence keenly.

I'm in a ward with three other old men. I don't listen to their conversations, which aren't loud, and what I have overheard was mainly personal. I may have missed some political talk, which is a relief in this time of Brexit/Johnson/Trump opinion. I read Barry Lopez, re-read *Word and Stone*, do quick crosswords, WRITE. In this situation, I've been writing with surprising fluency, words pouring out, ideas always ahead of me.

Looking back over the rush of poems of the other night, I think there are possibilities of shaping a few worthwhile things. This gives me a sense of being able to go on from *Word and Stone*.

24 June

Visit from Adele in the afternoon. She is a wise, loving woman, this old friend. She let me talk, become emotional, and talked sense to me.

It seems I'm not going to be out of here as soon as I hoped. While I feel quite well (apart from the inability to walk) doctors tell me my kidneys 'have taken a battering'. I remain outwardly cheerful, but have night-time (and daytime) fears.

I spent several hours working on the 'Addiction' story today, writing with fluency. I must never forget how much *escapes*. How could I give a full account of my life with M., or an accurate portrait of her? Yes, I write fluently, and honestly, but *life escapes*.

25 June

With a drip in my right arm, I was unable to write today. Long talk with Chris Meredith on the phone in the morning. *Resurgence*, with Peter Abbs's piece on *Ditch Vision*, arrived today. Peter's reading of the book goes deep. His response is a form of conversation.

26 June

Showered by an older nurse & a younger nurse. How I have lost my inhibitions! It's the nurses' naturalness that sets me free. And the shower was wonderful!

Visit from Byron & Eirlys, who bring me a notebook to write in, & two new books on Llewelyn Powys. Ceri Thomas visits too.

Emily & Joe come in in the evening. Elwin, who is 92, and once sang in the Treharris Male Voice Choir, sings quaveringly, in the bed opposite. I can barely understand him when he speaks to me. Elwin, with his white hair, and the remains of his singing voice, reminds me of my father. I remember Dad's 'I'm 90, Jerry, it's terrible'.

27 June

Bright, breezy morning. A memory of waking Jonathan Raban, before dawn, in the caravan in the vicarage garden, and going to Walhampton to fish for tench & carp. Bird voices & mist rising: sublime.

Pushed by physiotherapists through labyrinthine corridors to try some stairs (steps up to a platform). On the way we passed areas that I used to visit with M. for blood tests.

28 June

It was very touching this morning, when Elwin crossed the ward to apologize for keeping us awake with his noises in the night.

What one sees in a great hospital like this is the reality of democracy, with people caring, practically & with affection, for the old & the sick, and caring for them equally, intent on helping. At the same time, politicians jostle for position in the 'great world' outside (but affecting what happens here), *talking big*, making promises: a spectacle of, mostly, public schoolboys 'destined' from birth to lead.

Evening
Continued writing compulsion. Visit from Emily & Joe, who are busily re-arranging the house against my return, perhaps next week.

29 June

Another sleepless night, mind overworking. After breakfast (porridge & banana) Lauren gave me a bath, talking together all the while. I sing the praises of Prince Charles Hospital and tell the story, again, of our neglect in the other hospital when M. died.

Déjà vu. As in Frome, walking with a zimmer, lying in bed, sitting in a chair, receiving excellent care. But, here, I look out on an enormous yellow crane and men working on what I'm told are portacabins, close outside the ward, and, beyond, part of Merthyr rising to a hill ridge.

How different without M. And without those Wiltshire Downs Emily likes to think of me striding over, as I longed to do. No longer Old Schoolhouse to return to, or our morning walks. M. loved that house, its spaciousness & age. I loved it too, but it rarely haunts me, in spite of our life together there, and Mother's last weeks, and death. One of my happiest experiences was going home from hospital – *our* home – with paintings & sculptures & books.

> 'All great art tends to draw us out of ourselves.'
> Barry Lopez, *Horizon*

30 June

Call from Lee Grandjean in the afternoon. Very encouraging. All my loved ones are on my case. No neglecting my health again. I quoted the Lopez to Lee: it speaks my mind entirely, and is what I see in Lee's work. Of course, one would have to add that the artist has a self, and it's through the self that one draws energies, from nature, from the history of human life in relation to our surroundings, from the God-spark. David Jones distinguishes between the art of man-the-artist and the building of birds and bees. I think we are closer to non-human beings with our creativity.

1 July

Move from Ward 2 to Ward 7. Visit from Kay Cotton. Deep talk with my dear friend. Kay is a Quaker; our thought is similar about soul, spirit, breath of God. Kay believes firmly in life after death.

In a bed opposite, an old man looks almost dead. In my bed near the window, I look out over the carpark, remembering the many times we've searched for a parking space.

Evening visit from Joe & Holly, my granddaughter. Holly looking very attractive (like her mother). She's learning to drive in Southampton, as I did many years ago. We talked about animals, especially our love of donkeys. Joe has been so efficient in arranging the house against my return.

'Death, that forever famished and indifferent visitor, is more apparent in some places than others.'
Barry Lopez

2 July

Why has so much contemporary art lost the capacity 'to draw us out of ourselves' (Lopez)? Because it accepts – lives with – the limitations of the prevailing (Western) culture. We are being talked and entertained to death, our relationships commodified, our life purposes defined in exclusively material terms. *This is the age of the private ego.* Ego as end in itself, without depth, and essentially isolated from other egos, or in competition with them. Sex is treated widely as ego exchange. (Lawrence understood this well and strove to redefine/reimagine sexual relationships. The mistake he made was to preach to women.) *We lack connection* – comprehensively – to one another, to nature, to God.

In this situation the naturalists & poet-naturalists are fighting back. This is the time of eco-poetry, of poets who write in the spirit of Rachel Carson, Barry Lopez & others. This follows the time of confessionalism, in which poets were intensely concerned with their selves (and, often, wrongs other people had done them). *This was poetry of the bruised ego.*

There's action & reaction, excessive inwardness leading to outward-ness, that risks losing the human soul. Instead of exclusiveness, we need to look at spiritual being in the human and non-human world.

It seems to be a cooler day today with puffball clouds. I am again in a room with three men, but here I sense one or more is close to death. While I feel much better, I'm suddenly afraid of dying, especially at night. Closeness to death makes me realize how suddenly all our thoughts & works & sense of self can be *gone.*

Evening

Walked to the phone for a good talk with Elin. Connor Tan, the carer who accompanied me, was a young Welsh/Chinese lad. I told him about Amy Tan.

In lectures, I used to describe Edward Thomas's 'I' as the most personal among English poets. I think I would hold to that. I meant it as praise, and still would, qualifying praise with criticism of an excessive self-consciousness in some poems. I think I first met his poetry in school, with 'The Manor Farm, which became for me emblematic of a particular mood of the English countryside. When I became aware of its date, 1916, I began to think more critically of Thomas in his England, and the difference between rural ideal and warring Empire.

It is apparent that for Edward Thomas nature was a *partial* drawing out of self. Hence, together with his use of some words with religious connotations, his description by some (e.g., Richard Harries) as a religious poet.

Ted Hughes's remark that Thomas was 'father of us all' (later English poets) makes me uneasy. Tony Conran saw the danger of Thomas worship among Anglo-Welsh poets & others. (And, yes, that would have included me.) Of course, the crucial figure for me is David Jones, in whom I recognised a poet of native (British) depths, and a breaker of narrow forms, and an exciting experimental Modernist, 'experiment' with Jones relating closely to his Catholic (incarnational) vision.

Pursuing this line of thought now, I would celebrate Lawrence, especially *Birds, Beasts and Flowers* and *Last Poems,* and acknowledge (as he did) his debt to Whitman. For me, Lawrence, especially in *Last Poems,* is a great religious poet, and I could not complete my book on Poetry & the Sacred without discussing him. This also would be a link to eco-poetry, which expresses a particular understanding of the sacred. There is a spirit that animates poetry which draws us out of ourselves.

This is Christian in some poets (e.g. Smart, Vaughan, Eliot), but even Christian poets tend to deploy pagan (nature) elements, and poets tend to be polytheistic, invoking pagan influences, as Milton does. How could they not, when the Bible (OT & NT) comes out of a semi-pagan world?

I'm sure Lopez is right. If we don't draw ourselves out of ourselves, we neglect the life of relationship, without which nothing really exists.

The thing about lyric poetry is that it's feeling. No theory can deny that, unless it negates its very subject. This is where the problem has arisen for me in all my thinking/worrying about ego, Self, and self-transcendence. If lyric poetry is feeling, it is personal. The question, then, is what is the person? Not the ego alone, certainly. One etymology is 'speaking through' ('persona' or mask). I like this: it implies possibility of opening to the depths, which I deem to be both personal and common. Certainly, poetry that draws us out of ourselves speaks of a shared sense of the reality of life in the universe.

In all of this, I feel my way.

3 July

I was hoping to go home today, but while care at home is being put in place, I shall be staying here. I want to go home. I've so much to write up, and it will be much more convenient for Joe.

The old man opposite, with open mouth, as we are in our extremity, reminds me of the effigy of skeletal Bishop Fox in Winchester Cathedral, which frightened me as a boy, and always chilled me.

Would we benefit now from representing ourselves with a Dance of Death? People in the Third World wouldn't need to. But we in the West still sanitize death, even hide it away, or diminish its existential reality with commercials for funeral plans.

Animism/Paganism is, for me, the challenge to Christianity. An element in my attraction to Christianity is the pastoral world of Christ's time, and his language of mustard seed, etc. Paganism shares with Christianity the language of nature but embodies nature's generative, sexual energy. The Pagan sees the life force in a lily or a rose, the Christian an emblem or symbol of purity. Lust (not violence) is sacred in Blake, who was no orthodox Christian, but the poet who made a form of Christianity possible for later English poets. Keats, also, with the holiness of the heart's

19

affections, and the conversation of sparrows. I feel this link back, through Modernism & American poetry in the Emersonian tradition, and very little sympathy with post-Larkin English verse, in spite of being moved by Larkin's lyricism.

We have to be capable of admiration, hero-worship, even. We have to love poetry before we begin to think we might be poets. And then, beginning, we have to shake off envy and know that poetry isn't a competition. Otherwise it becomes an ego adjunct, and we never draw ourselves out of ourselves.

At this point, Helen, a nurse from the Rhondda, remarks on my writing and pauses to question me and enter into conversation.

Evening

Bernard Harrington visits, bringing me a sequence of his poems, 'Colliery', based on his experience as an engineer inspecting mines. Poems about real things, intelligent, ironic, caring.

A lovely night with clear sky. I can imagine making the last cast of the day on the river above the Shallows, landing my fly in shadow under the trees – unwilling to pack up my tackle and leave. Or reeling in my line from the lower lake at Walhampton, or Pylewell. Anticipation to the last, sadness, & frustration at having to leave. Or I might be starting at Hurst, under the castle walls, excited to cast into the 'hole', just off the shingle bank, with West Wight & the Needles across the water. Days & nights that seemed out of time, since I had no real sense of an end.

4 July

Jim, a nurse, tells me that his father flew in Lancasters during the war, and survived a crash in which four men died. Caring for his father in his last years was what decided Jim to become a nurse.

Paul, in the next bed, is going home today. I thought he was a young man until we talked. He worked in the Taff Merthyr Vale colliery for 30 years. So, another hospital day begins for us at 6 a.m. Later, I hear fragments of a discussion of Lorca, with Melvyn Bragg, on the radio.

There are long weary hours in hospital. I could sleep now, but resist going back to bed. I read, listen to music, enjoying some lovely pieces by Schubert & Mozart. I've written a lot, more than in any comparable period: many poems, and a large part of the Addiction story. I remember the sleepless night of the solstice, when I wrote poem after poem. I think I was in an observation room, by myself, for perhaps two nights before that. But my memory of the period when I felt so weak is vague.

I want to be at home with Joe, contacting Emily & friends (so many thankyous to write), ordering books from Tony Frazer, writing up poems. Beginning what will be a new life, initially downstairs. Oh, and seeing the cats!

In *Horizon* Barry Lopez describes meeting Arvo Pärt, and the effect on him of Pärt's music. Pärt's wife explains to Lopez 'that what her husband composes can reassemble a person'. This is perhaps the greatest claim for art's potential effect that I've met. I know that it's true. The operative word is '*re*-assemble', which implies a previous state of disintegration, that is often our common human condition.

5 July

A cooler morning, cloudy with rifts of pale blue sky. The summer is passing outside, registered in here by window views, and some nights when heat makes it difficult to sleep. A woman has been screaming in the corridor, but her screaming stopped early last night. The man in the bed opposite must be close to death. When I hear him talking/crying out in the night, there's a terrible loneliness in his voice. It shakes me to think that I could end like that, utterly weak, and with no control of bodily functions, no possibility of 'reassembling' myself. Nurses speak to him kindly as they change and feed him and he is scarcely able to respond. Some nurses call us 'boy' or 'boyo' (quite *Under Milk Wood*!). In this hospital, I feel the warm, practical humanity that is the life of South Wales, grown in the communities in which suffering & fellowship have 'forged' (that industrial metaphor!) a people. Humanity is palpable here.

After breakfast: Irregular heartbeat following low blood count. Anxiety, a hit to my confidence, but I work on 'A Dreaming' which helps to calm me. A new poem can be *a kind of imaginative field of force.*

21

Afternoon: Back to Ward 2, because of morning ECG. Greeted by Elwin, who sings softly to himself. Beside the window, I have a rather different view, but similar hills behind hospital buildings & houses. A nurse I find especially attractive seems genuinely pleased to see me back. We old fools! We desire until we're dead.

When my mind is working as a poet it's a field of force, a generative energy, which will seize on particular words & images. A lot of the work is done in this way, with ego quiescent, and material drawn in/emanating from diverse sources. It's a kind of specialisation, I suppose, which made me seem dumb as a boy (e.g. failing 11-Plus), and stupid with regard to other forms of knowledge, such as languages, science, music.

How strange are workings of the mind, which some specialists see as a function of the brain. Oh, I hope not! How depressed I was by that spirit-killing book, *The Mind in the Cave*. What I intuit is embodiment, with mind at the tips of senses, and creative with memory as well as imagination.

I've argued against the idea of poet as specialist, and espoused the Wordsworthian 'man' speaking to 'men', and voice of place. But this is rather different: poetry is a gift, and an art. It can take many forms, but lyric poetry voices feeling. Which doesn't mean it stops thought, only poetic thinking is different from philosophy, theology, etc, however much it draws on them.

We are relational, embodied beings in a world of bodies, or persons, as an animist would say. Our minds aren't locked in our skulls, in spite of the boundary we can't cross, between person and person. We have the equivalent of mycorrhizal fungi, a network of threads, like trees. We are deeply *in* the world, and a poet's knowledge and way of thinking and perceiving taps into the world he/she is part of. Wordsworth's thinking was limited by his idea of 'Man'. A poet is a liminal being in more than one sense, including gender.

I understand well why Lee wants to make things that have never been seen before. I would like to make poems like that. I find much to agree with in Eliot's 'Tradition and the Individual Talent', an essay written by a young, exploratory poet trying to locate his innovative verse – which would have surprised him, as new poetry does – in relation to traditional (mainly European) poetry. He was thinking of the beginnings of art too, as we must.

Afternoon

Visit of nice, middle aged Irish Dr Nolan. I'm waiting for another ECG to check on this morning's mysterious increased heartbeat.

Looking out the window, I see a flight of pigeons or doves, caught by the sun. The wheeling birds make me think of Idris Davies, a poet I now associate with the Gelligaer moorland above Rhymney. I'd like to write a poem in his honour.

Evening

Visit from Joe. Phone call from Elin, who has been dreaming of Mieke. In one dream M. tried to push her off a cliff which Elin interpreted as telling her to come to me in Wales. Across the North Sea: journeys that became part of my life over 4-5 years.

Anticipation's the thing! Could it all really be more than 30 years ago that I met M.? So much lives with me, as if 'yesterday' didn't exist.

I look across the ward to Elwin who bears some resemblance to my father and remember visiting Dad in the nursing home, when I was the man Joe now is, fit & taking responsibility. At times, the passage of time is like a sudden landslide. At other times, we savour the years ... I guess that at the moment of death, for a conscious mind, life, however long it has been, slides past. And there is no time. We are in eternity now, Jefferies said. He could feel the opposite too, when he thought of the earth he loved vanishing, as if it had never existed. That's the haunting thought. George Fox was tormented by the idea that everything comes by nature (and therefore goes, so what of the inner light?). He overcame the tormenting thought, and became the man we know, fierce in defence of the spiritual light.

There's a mood in which I can think, seeing myself and the other old men around me, all so tender of ourselves, what's the fuss? We're only dying, and if it be not now, yet it will come. Consider the multitude who have passed through this world, including the uncountable number who have passed today, and are passing now. A mood, but each of us so singular, alive & desiring life (unless desperately sick). Death, the common visitor, will remain most fearsome.

Light beginning to fade, not die, one living shade replaced by another. How little we appreciate this rhythm of night & day, the wonder of it, which we grow up to take for granted. Then, perhaps, comes some existential shock, and for a time we see.

A gull flies past in the fading light, and, with it, I sense the presence of the River Taff flowing through Merthyr and down to Cardiff and the sea.

Turning on my radio at night, I hear, through its crackling, Philip Gross's voice. He's reading one of his Pylons poems and discussing the word 'common' with Ian McMillan and a woman poet whose name I don't catch. I think Philip a fine poet, and one of our most intelligent, a rapid thinker, with access to a wide range of surprising contemporary material & metaphor. We became friends partly through concern for 'our addicts', as we called them: a close member of his family, with anorexia, and my Mieke. As poets we are quite different, yet have important affinities in the questions we ask and address.

Where I am now as a poet is where I want to be. I want to go on from here.

6 July

Afternoon visiting time on a clouded day. No one for me today. Two elderly women & a man sit with Elwin, who occasionally seems to fall asleep, mouth open, but obviously welcomes company. Sometimes we say a few friendly words to each other – I told him I enjoyed his singing – but I'm apprehensive when he calls to me, because afraid of not understanding. Looking through the window along the line of hills I see a pyramid shape that is surely a reclaimed slag heap. It's hard to imagine Merthyr as it was in the age of coal & iron & steel, when it was a furnace of energy, and a disgrace to Victorian humanity, yet also a place of great heroism among some professional men as well as working men, women & children.

At a spare moment, a nurse, Andrea, asks to read my poems and takes up the book. I say: 'Don't feel you have to say anything', as I always do in similar circumstances. Not to patronise: I know how tongue-tied one can become faced with modern art or music, or poetry. Even a professional reader (e.g. teacher of creative writing) has sometimes to fall back on words that mean little, such as 'interesting', while hoping to find a more helpful response.

I learnt a lot from teaching creative writing. But, finally, it tired me, and I felt I was giving to others energy, and concentration, that I needed for my own poetry. Hence my pleasure at returning to teach literature at the University of Glamorgan. A move I made also in the hope of helping Mieke to combat her addiction. Teaching over more than 40 years took a lot of my energy. But what a privilege it was: 'paid', as we would sometimes say, 'to read books we love'.

The Scottish lady comes around, bringing tea. 'Scotland the brave,' says Elwin.

Occasionally, when writing furiously these days (especially on the solstice night, when I was ill), I've felt that I might do myself a mental injury, and it would be better to stop. But this is what I was meant to do – the thing growing in the mind – the being – of the inchoate, inarticulate boy. And in any case, I'm not writing *all* the time. But my mind is a magnet, a field of force, and almost any word can suddenly light up. It's the opposite of writer's block, and of the poem – the non-poem – overwritten to death. In the past, when teaching, I would stifle an embryonic poem by postponement.

After supper, Andrea helps me back into bed. I've sat up in the chair longer today.

I lie in bed, a Mozart opera playing in my ear. Elwin sits in his chair, head resting on his hand. He is such an old man, his white hair like my father's. Cloud lies on the landscape outside, the Welsh Trade Centre glowing like an ember on the hill.

The temptation of a diary is to try to write everything as it happens. Impossible, of course; yet a temptation to write instead of live.

Trust life and it will lay down a kind of mould from which new creative life can grow. On rare occasions, I've felt my diary to be a burden, and a barrier against experience, and with that risk of introspection – self-absorption – coming between me and those I love. Very occasionally, I've given it up for a time. But it is truly a friend, and one that can sometimes call me to account.

Beware the life of monologue.

I wonder how many of the poems I've written in hospital I'll be able to retrieve, revise, make publishable. Some, certainly. This period has been a creative release – because I felt close to death? In part, perhaps. But there is also the freedom to write. Not only this, though. A stream of thinking and feeling, a lyrical stream, has been released in my mind.

7 July

No sleep until the early hours. Elwin was restless and making a lot of noise, groaning, talking to himself, shouting out. When at last I slept, I dreamt of trying to give a talk on Hardy to the Vaughan Colloquium and, failing to find my notes, *ad libbing*, and apologising profusely for my lack of professionalism.

Listening to a radio poem, 'Borderlands', by a woman of Chinese/Jamaican descent, I'm reminded how exciting radio can be for a poet. Also, how rich we are now in potential for new poetry, by poets bringing diverse cultural & linguistic influences into the English language. By comparison, I am an old-timer. But one can only work authentically in 'the parish of one's care'. None of us is universal man or woman. Remember Patrick Kavanagh & W.C.W.

8 July

Good night's sleep.

Poetry is lifework, and if authentic it has the stamp of the poet's being, his or her 'soul'. It makes the soul visible – tangible? We speak of poetic 'landscapes' without necessarily meaning specific areas, though sometimes we do, e.g. 'Housman country'. The particular makes the national, Irishness, Englishness, etc. Thus, poets help us to know who we are.

This knowledge may increase awareness of difficulty and confusion. An English poet, now, is marginal, with a troubling imperial history and an uncertain present. From a poetic point of view, this means opportunity, possibility. We are *entangled*, to use Geoffrey Hill's suggestive word, and out of our entanglement, we write.

Another hospital day, another week. I sit at my table writing, as I wait for a nurse to give me a shower. I am so much better than when I was admitted, but not very mobile. Will I need to get used to a zimmer way of life?

I want to work forward, opening myself to the unexpected, as well as tackling certain long thought of ambitions, which it would be dangerous for me to name. I was always a slow starter. Now I am in haste.

Anxiety about egotism has inhibited me, at the same time as the struggle with ego makes for a form of autobiography! How much we would have lost if we didn't have Keats's letters, or if Wordsworth had been less self-involved in *The Prelude*, or Milton less of an egotist, as Coleridge described him. This world is the place of soul-making, as Keats said.

Early on at Aberystwyth, I immersed myself in Keats's work. I lectured to a first-year class in the wonderful West Room, which looked out on the sea, beyond the broken-down pier. On wild days, with the sea roaring and a gale blasting against the windows, it was a dramatic place to be. In Winchester, Keats virtually became a neighbour, since he'd lived so intensely there. For me, it's love that makes a hero. I mean the capacity to love, manifested in life & work. Hence my first real attraction to the Powyses was through Llewelyn's letters, which are so loving, especially to J. C. P & other family members. In those letters I found an emotional release. Thus, poetry can set us free to love. Perhaps this is its greatest gift: love of others, love of life, love of poetry itself.

Doctor Nolan comes to question me, concerned about the episode of heart arrhythmia, which hasn't recurred. I am 6 on a scale of 9 for risk of stroke or heart attack. When she asks me if I have any questions, I say no, but I have a remark. I compliment her on the beautiful, colourful blouse she's wearing today. She responds with pleasure and I notice the doctors & nurses accompanying her exchanging glances and smiles.

Not knowing is a principle with me, but first it is an instinct; it speaks who I am, how I experience. My life has been rich in love & friendship. I've come close to certain people, but always I've been aware of the ultimate barrier: the skin that is actual and spiritual. It could be experienced as a condemnation to ultimate isolation, but without it there can be no love, only self-love. In love, I think what matters most is trust, not fidelity alone, but recognising and valuing the other as other. We meet most closely, I feel, in sharing something that is not ourselves: music, a poem, walking in a wood or by the sea, "ditch vision". The psychological way, talking about oneself or trying to describe inner experience, tempts us into the maze, the labyrinth that is also a hall of mirrors, from which we emerge exhausted, probably self-sick, and no wiser. I believe in therapy (how could I not, when I was married to a healer?) and I understand that many people have benefited from psychiatric treatment, but I distrust the modern world of psychiatry & psychology. Freud & Jung were both great storytellers: myth-makers. They brought light into our modern world. But they created systems, and no system can encompass or penetrate the mystery of the human soul.

Afternoon: A porter runs me through the hospital for an Echo Cardiogram (uncomfortable) & ECG. Through the department where M. and I would sit waiting for a blood test. A glimpse through a door of the outer world – how good it looks, sunny & fresh even though the day is overcast. I live on window views, but they have their limitations.

The obituary of a sculptor, Michael Lyons, describes him as 'one of the group of artists who developed successful careers from a non-metropolitan base'. What a scandal it is that non-metropolitan artists should have to struggle because of their 'provincial' situation. Yet, often, living and working outside London, being outside the 'game', stimulates vital work. Trendiness is mainly a metropolitan phenomenon. In recent years, it has stifled artistic creativity in England. London is a marvellous, world city, but arts in England are dying from influence of the metropolitan base and its narrowness.

Elwin at 92, is failing, but still completely himself. He has a son of 70. We exchange friendly words, not always coherently.

After 7.30 in the evening, anxious for a nurse to come to help me back into bed. Today, I've been sitting in my chair since breakfast time. Only a day or two ago I was back in bed between 1 and 2, feeling tired. Switching on the radio, I catch part of a programme in which children are talking about living with alcoholic parents. Heartbreaking, the anger, the frustration, the neglect, the hopeless attempt to understand, the pity of it all.

9 July

Wake to more idiocy on the world stage. Trump. Who else? How could American democracy fall so low? Big business. Big talk. Big boasts & promises.

After breakfast I do the foot & leg exercises the physios showed me. Truth is, I'm easily bored with exercise. Lazy. Eager to get back to my writing & books. But this is probably why I'm in here.

A doctor refers to a narrowing of a vein close to my heart. Common, she says, in people of my age.

Lunch time. Elwin is so like my father, asleep with mouth open, or as Dad was when I would feed him and he would open his mouth like a little bird. Towards the end, if we are still ourselves, our whole lives are in our mind, sometimes muddled, sometimes preternaturally clear. M. & I would visit Dad regularly in the nursing home. We were then in the midst of life.

As I age, I see more often, and more clearly, the boy I was: hypersensitive, unformed, telling myself stories in which I was a hero, then tormented by the onset of puberty, when I knew nothing about sex. Aged 10 or 11, I was writing my first Jefferies-inspired nature sketches, and beginning to discover modern poetry. I craved friendship. And when I discovered angling, my life was transformed. I kept a diary of my fishing, copying a Bernard Venables image of a pike onto the cover. Then, or shortly after, I had begun to read Hardy's novels, but Jefferies' essays came first. My great good fortune, along with love, was that poems & paintings & music (mainly song) were as natural in the house as vegetables & fruit in the garden. It's hard for me to really feel what was happening in the world at that time. At first, the war was the world. As an adult, I came to value highly the work of the Attlee government, and to be deeply moved by art of the time, such as Humphrey Jennings' films.

Part walking, part shuffling back to my chair, I remember the old lady in the nursing home saying to me with a sweet smile, as she walked past very slowly, 'Someone is going past called S-N-A-I-L'.

Evening. Harry Christophers' The Sixteen from York Minster. Sublime sacred music. Surely, the distinctive voice of Elin Manahan Thomas, my friend Wynn's daughter. But all are angelic. Can one hear such music and imagine it vanishes into an empty heaven? Jack Clemo thought jazz was God's music. One would suppose that if there is a God, he would welcome all good music. Flippancy can't live with this sublime sound. Long applause: so, this is an entertainment. Is that what Taverner & MacMillan compose for? Surely not. But an entertainment can reassemble us, if not reach God.

10 July

Any day could be the day I go home. Lying in bed last night, I realised that I risk being institutionalised. It is, after all, rather comfortable here.

Poems are still working in my mind – phrases, revisions – but more slowly, although any word, read or spoken or thought, can suddenly feel magnetic. As long as I live, the field of force will exist with its potential, sometimes somnolent, at other times apparently non-existent. It can be activated (up to a point) or suppressed. As a teacher, I had often to suppress it, thinking I was postponing a poem – which vanished, or lingered as a ghost. Some poems that were embryonic long ago have been born in recent years. The mind is always more of a whole than we are conscious of, and more creative. Our age is achieving huge progress in many directions, but also devising more ways of stifling the mind. Poetry speaks human. And human is relational.

Christopher Middleton was right. We are living through a death of the imagination. Christopher saw English poetry in our time participating in the death. He was too sweeping; but I fear many poets & publishers don't know what he meant.

ECG machine misbehaving, so I lie in bed, stickers attached to my body making me feel like Gulliver.

Young Sophie bathes me. Nurses call me 'Jer', occasionally 'Boy', or 'Lovely', as they do other older patients. I should be going home this afternoon. I thank Dr Nolan & her attendant nurses, telling them how wonderful they are.

Tony Curtis visits and we just have time for a good talk before the ambulance is ready to take me home. This is an annoying journey because the young St John's ambulance man talks all the time about his prowess as a referee on the football field: a real authoritarian, handing out red & yellow cards. He shows no interest in me.

Back home, Joe, with Emily's help, has transformed the living room into a bedroom & work space for me, and has had the walls painted. He couldn't have arranged things better. Settling in, I have a sudden, acute sense of Mieke's absence.

To WCW

I find it is true:
any thing is worthy of a poem,
if poetry is worth a thing.

2.

28 August

A relapse has brought me back into hospital. I was in bed feeling unwell when Debbie & Ian visited yesterday afternoon. Overnight I stayed clothed in a wet bed. Fortunately, Emily visited in the morning and called an ambulance car. Mandy, the driver, got me into the car, and out of it at the hospital, with difficulty. I'm a dead weight.

I've now been here two days feeling low and heavy. The bacterial infection has recurred and I'm fitted with a catheter and have drips in my arms. To my relief, Joe visited me with Harry this morning, from their caravan holiday in Pembrokeshire. He brought me books and writing materials and a mobile phone, and good cheer. I write now with lifted spirits, in a single room on Ward 4. I have been dozing, and when awake, turning poems over in my mind.

On the afternoon of my admittance Bernard visited. He is a faithful friend. In these lonely hours I hold accounting with myself, running over things done ill, but also taking pleasure in love given & received, and work achieved. I don't feel ready to die. This time last year Mieke was in her final days.

29 August

An uncomfortable night with little sleep. I don't feel well. Sitting in a chair at midday, but I can't stand without help. Whatever the condition, it's distressing.

Scraps of poems in the evening. Mind working again.

30 August

I've been diagnosed with osteomyelitis (infection in the bone). Catheter taken out, brings some relief. Got stuck in the toilet this morning due to lack of staff.

1 September

Bad night. Morning a little better, when I sat in chair. Despondent when Emily rang, I stupidly spoke of not wanting to live as I am. The feeling passes. I wonder if M. knew she was going to die, and whether, suffering so much, she welcomed death. I know how that might be.

Reading Anne Wroe's *Facets of Light*, a lovely book. Light in the landscape – a kind of spiritual beauty in effects of sunlight, birdsong – seems to be a very English kind of experience, linking poets & painters, irrespective of their religious persuasion, or lack of one: Ravilious, Palmer, Blake, Coleridge, Edward Thomas, Clare, Jefferies, Hudson... It does include Americans, however, especially Thoreau, and the Welsh R.S. Thomas.

This is a tradition I love, and being reminded of it in my present sickness is restorative. But I've far to go.

Jefferies was among the greatest of these visionaries because he saw the wheat was beautiful, but knew human life is labour. He knew how England treated its labouring people. So did Blake, prophet against Empire. And Clare, who suffered the treatment. There is no true way except the way of double vision: aesthetic/spiritual, and political. To see light only is sentimental. To see only darkness is spiritless.

2 September

Bad night. Breathing difficult. Oxygen in morning. Low, but doctor reassuring, & good messages: Emily, Joe, Bethan, Chris Meredith. Letter from Stevie Davies with her friend Andrew's warm appreciation of *Word and Stone*. Heart lifting.

3 September

In this ward we are old men – at any time, 3 or 4 – in various stages of dissolution. One leaves for another ward; another old man arrives. Several are evidently in worse conditions than me. Immobility apart, I don't feel so bad today, and snooze, or read Séan Street's new book, *The Sound inside the Silence*, or listen to music on Radio 3, currently Bruckner's 8th Symphony. This makes me think of a cathedral of sound, in 'space' that contains powerful, turbulent emotions, but does *contain* them, and with a gentle, quiet lyricism emerging or breaking in. The making of the world might be conceived as a kind of music, as also a painting with light. It would be terrible, thunderous, the dark struck through – too dreadful for any human ear – yet within the noise & darkness, sweet sounds, like little birds singing over a battlefield.

Earlier, an older nurse told me in no uncertain terms that the Remainers had manipulated the Brexit vote. The Leavers were entirely truthful. She saw a civil war coming and knew which side she would be on. Disturbing, this sudden descent from pleasant chat with a person one finds helpful and amiable, into bigoted slanging.

Late afternoon. Two nurses, John & Kai, get me out of bed. Kai, who's always cheery, is from the Philippines. So is Sandy, a male night nurse, who moves quietly, appears suddenly, and always startles me, which makes us laugh.

4 September

Feeling flat. Physical? Mental? No apparent progress towards mobility. This flesh! What we all are, some more, some less. Inescapable except when dead. Flesh: enemy of poetry? It simply dulls the spirit. Yet when we are fit and strong, our flesh, which is also our senses, sings.

Trolleyed through corridors for ultra sound scan on arteries of right leg.

5 September

It has dawned on me that I am likely to be in hospital for some weeks. This morning I walked a few steps with zimmer & physios – scarcely more than a bed length. At least I am out of bed this morning, sitting in a chair and have had a wash. But I shall need to adapt. When Joe brings me a laptop it will make a difference.

Lunchtime call from Fiona Owen in Anglesey. I need some of Fiona's Buddhist wisdom to sustain me. The physical condition of the three old men with me in this ward is worse than mine. Their mental states seem to be much worse, and they're seldom able to communicate. To the nurses, young & older, we must be like old babies, some of us needing enticing to eat or drink or speak, and all needing *looking after*. They are under-staffed, under pressure, but work steadily, without complaint.

7 September

Colin, old man with injured head, in bed opposite, is scarcely coherent. In the night he shouts for Linda, his wife. I cry out silently for Mieke. A nurse, giving me insulin late at night, is close to tears. Overwork here is terrible.

Bernard came in, thoughtfully bringing me postcards from 'home'. Views of Lymington, Keyhaven, New Forest, Mudeford, Christchurch, Rockford Common. These caused me a twinge, but mostly because I remembered the period of writing *Solent Shore* and the ache to return south, when each place name was a poem. I almost feel that these places have nothing to do with me now, or I have nothing to do with them, especially now that Jim, my main link with the area, is dead. One has to be realistic. There's feeling for one's native place, and there's place with its own agenda: functions, house prices, social hierarchies, etc. Love is an unnecessary extra. I've always known this; it's been the wall I've beaten my head against. I've written a 'poetry of place' that the place, one or two individuals apart, doesn't recognise. I have been badly hurt and it sounds as if I'm bitter. In fact, whatever I've achieved as a writer has depended upon my failure to realise the early dream, which spoke the heart and mind of a man unwilling to grow up.

Another hospital day begins with these reflections. Sunday, an understaffed, quiet day. Joe is with Chloe photographing a friend's wedding in a field at or near Tisbury in Wiltshire, which I told him was our ancestral ground. I imagine all those labouring generations and the world or worlds they knew! Even my parents began life in the age of horses. I've always felt that I live partly in that other world, with an instinctive slowness and need to feel close to the soil, and that I've gone wrong in my mind when most removed from it, with no mud on my shoes. Most of what is good in my life has come from touch: human contact, material imagination (e.g. Lee's sculptures), and nature, ground. No good at logical thought, and hopeless with all technology, I need things, especially natural things, to think with. I know the drawbacks, but I know too how much we need poetry of touch, at a time when we increasingly live in our heads, abstracted from things of Earth.

9 September

Drafting new poems: 'Kuzula', 'Night Thoughts', 'Symphony', 'Escape'.

10 September

A step forward, walking with the 'pulpit' across the ward and ready to graduate to zimmer. Good talk with Lee.

Anne Wroe's fine *Six Facets of Light* is rather too much of a good thing. She weaves into her narrative many quotations from visionary writers & artists, including Palmer & Blake. These are beautiful, inspiring, but are torn from the context of lives that knew struggle, and in some cases (e.g. Blake) were bitterly opposed to the prevailing spirit of their times. I want more of the existential life, with which I can feel more. 'Vision' in the modern world is acquired only through experience of encroaching dark. Meaning is won from meaninglessness. We can't take Blake out of politics, or politics out of Blake. He was an intellectual warrior and the war in which he fought continues today in a later phase.

11 September

More mobile. I sit in my dressing gown, in a chair by the bed, looking out at a misty early autumn day, the hills above Merthyr obscured. Beside me, in the new issue of *PN Review*, companionable poets, such as Andy Jordan and Jeff Wainwright, and the only book I could read when Mieke died, Donald Culross Peattie's *Flowering Earth*. How I want to understand the workings of the green world, to get into the processes of light & growth, to know the language of nature, and so renew and deepen my own poetic language. Through all phases, I have wanted to be a poet of the quick world – to tap into life, to speak the force I'm part of.

A young doctor, Anna, tells me I may be able to go home soon, with antibiotics. Then Joe rings: he's been up early getting housework done (before 10, like Nelly Dean, in *Wuthering Heights*, he always remembers her). I feel the way for a poet now – for me anyway – is deeper down, through life sciences, and farther out, life of spirit. God-light: that which *breaks in*, beyond our concepts & limited knowledge – spiritual life on the other side of words.

13 September

Warm morning. Blue sky with a little white cloud bringing out the line of the hill ridge above Merthyr. Letter from Kay Cotton containing a beautifully detailed poem. How I love poetry that gives me the world, which is also particular. Kay has been reading *Word and Stone*. She says: 'you speak from your Centre'.

This is what I would wish. Over years, I wrote about 'idea of the centre', influenced by *Celtic Heritage* and mindful of Yeats and 'The Second Coming', and thinking about writing *from* place. 'Centre' spoke my sense of the value of every life in each particular locality, and my opposition to the influence of 'popular' culture. Then, I thought less of writing from the heart, because in thrall to an idea of impersonality. It's only gradually that I've come to understand that I'm a lyric poet – which means an emotional, sensing being in the world.

As autumn comes on, I hunger for a touch of things, if only to stand in the garden by the birch and rowan trees looking across the valley at the hills. To feel a breeze in my face, and perhaps rain. While I can look out of the window, the hospital is like a cocoon, warm, all-embracing, airless. It saves lives, but one has to be out to enjoy the sensation of life. In the end, a poet's legacy, however philosophical or metaphysical, is what he or she has sensed.

14 September

Another lovely, late summer day of what I would probably be calling Hambledon weather if I were outdoors. Some times in our lives have an aura, an almost tangible sense of a time in time, and out of time, in which our feelings are bound up with place & weather & season. That's how the season at Child Okeford in 1969 was for me: the Hambledon days, when I was all raw nerves but beginning to mend, with a passion for that country which took me out of myself.

It's early afternoon; two old men in this ward are asleep, mouths open. One of them cried out in pain last night. All of us are old, but I seldom feel old, in spite of disability. I do feel bored at times, which is quite rare for me these days. What worries me is that my condition may recur and become worse. I visualise losing a foot or limb, like Jim, whom I think about a lot, as I do M. It seems such a short time since we were all together.

In the evening, Joe visits with Paula and her little daughter, Coco. A man across the ward – Derek – shouts most of the time: *Help me Nurse Nurse Help me Someone Help me.* Nurses come to help but are clearly fed up with him. But we can't measure another's pain or despair. My neighbour, Bryn, with whom I talk a little, is a nice old man. Bryn's wife of 60 years died 5 years ago. He thinks of her all the time, as I think of M., consciously, or under other thoughts.

As I write, a glorious sunset flares up behind the ridge.

15 September

Mid-September. Hospital routines continue, not quite seamlessly, due to staff shortages. Mercifully for him, and for his ward mates, Derek slept last night, and is asleep now. I would not like to lose mental control. I remember being told about the last days of a famous writer, everyone's idea of an English gentleman, how nasty he became. In extremity, we are all capable of becoming monsters: nothing but ravening egos, afraid, or hungry for the peace of painless sleep.

I feel quite well most of the time now, and in sight of the mobility I had before the relapse. I sense, though, that with antibiotics a further relapse is being kept at bay. Out of bed in my chair, I lose myself in writing & reading & quick crosswords, but have periods of discontent, when I look out of the window and long to be Emily's Dad, as she remembers me, striding over the hills. The rush of poems hasn't recurred, but I have a few fragments to work with. I think how M. would be here for me if she were alive, and wonder about the possibility of some form of life after death. As Alun Lewis felt, what concerns us is the fate of the beloved. Our minds are too small to conceive what might be. Humans dream of eternal life, but what we actually know is finitude. Poets console themselves with the thought of a sort of afterlife in other minds, but we are very Claudios at the prospect of death.

16 September

Routine of another hospital week begins. Low blood sugar count, but I don't feel bad effects.

In Anne Wroe's book, I love a Constable study of clouds which depicts buzzards wheeling against a white maelstrom. It's hard to say why this is exciting, except that it captures the life of birds in their dynamic element: an aspect of this animate universe.

Yet, for me, there is a surfeit of beauty in this book. Or, perhaps I should say, optimism about the human subject. How decisively Goethe said to Eckermann: 'There is nothing without us that is not also within us'. Human sovereignty, the divine spark, scarcely survives our understanding of the human place in the natural world: that great humbling, which is also an influx of fellow feeling, that followed Darwin's revolution. Ultimately, it's a question of what one can *feel*, and what one can think. Visionaries such as Traherne & Hopkins saw God, the divine light, in the human & natural world. This is what is now hard to see – for many, impossible. I stand precariously on a tottering bridge …

But what matters for an artist is not theological certainty, but the quality, the quickness, of his or her works. Our business is *sensing* - not concepts or system building. There are good reasons why very few poets, painters or musicians are philosophers, and most of those who were, lived in an age of faith. Poetic thinking is a reality, but it usually works through doubt & uncertainty, as well as insight & sensation, as Keats, one of our truest thinkers, knew.

Afternoon

Derek, across the room, is calling repeatedly for help. Nurses come and go, attempting to relieve his pain by moving him. A doctor has told me that my antibiotics are being changed for tablets. Depending upon the effect, I should soon – but how soon? – be allowed to go home. The treatment is not without risks.

Good talk with Philip yesterday. Messages from Liz Mathews & Tony Curtis.

17 September

A year today since Mieke's funeral. Sunflowers all the way.

At times, I almost lose my head with Derek's shouting, day & night. I could walk across the room and strangle him. Yesterday afternoon he and his son were shouting at each other, I sympathised with the young man's exasperation.

Physiotherapists, Ross & lovely Georgia, took me to try the 'stairs' (a few steps up, turn on platform and descend) this morning. I found this exercise scary when trying it on my first hospitalisation earlier this year. This time it was quite easy, suggesting that I'll soon be able to go home.

In this blessed hour, Derek is asleep. When not nervously enraged, I see a huge pathos in his constant demands, which ignore everyone but himself. We're all capable of howling from agony or loss.

Reading Séan's book and fiddling with drafts of poems, another beautiful day passing outside. I'm feeling well enough now to worry about my big, bushy beard, which makes me feel like Robinson Crusoe. My father had a prejudice against men with beards, possibly because he saw them as pseudo-artists, or echoing his father's philistinism.

A cheering call from Emily in the evening, promising a visit. It's been a pleasantly quiet day apart from Derek's shouting. Joe sent me a video of his drive over the moors from Tredegar which reminded me of the raw beauty of the area, and made me long for the open air.

18 September

A doctor and podiatrists visiting me this morning confirm my feeling that I'll be going home in a day or two. I've seen a lot of hospital this summer, enough to confirm my high regard for the struggling NHS, and enough for me.

Late afternoon sun. Sound of Derek shouting for help from the observation room. Apparently, he doesn't know where he is, though calling for nurses would suggest otherwise. I shan't forget his head sunk in pillows or his loud shouting. Initially unnerving, it became pathetic, and the atmosphere we live with in the ward.

Finished a draft of 'Symphony' and sent it to Séan.

The light of the setting sun behind the ridge suggests a chillier atmosphere. I look forward to going home, but also feel apprehensive of the long winter without M. Lights appear on the hill, the sky becomes a colder blue behind them. It is now after 7. Apart from a brief period on the bed, I have been sitting on my chair since before 7 in the morning.

27 September

In the end, I came out of hospital abruptly eight days ago. I was almost thrown out of 'my' bed, which was needed for another patient. Joe brought me home on an autumnal late afternoon and I entered the house feeling melancholy, because Mieke wasn't there. Since then, I've settled in fairly well. Philip visited yesterday and we were at once deep in serious conversation, pausing only to joke about having no small talk. Yellow and brown leaves among the remaining green on the rowan. Birch leaves scattered on the path outside the house.

Night in June

With curtains open
I lie in bed watching
the night come in.

Eyes of light flicker
where wind shakes leaves
on birches at the edge
of the quarry woods.

Dark presses in. I am heavy
wondering whether
this is the night
that I will die, and whether,

in death, you will greet me
or I too will be gathered in
and never see or think
of anything again.

I push back the bed clothes
and lie naked, feeling
the wind play over my skin.

I know that the air
which touches me
is moving among the leaves
that flicker in the dark

Under observation

I lie alone in a separate room.

It is night, but still the hospital
is busy with voices
and footsteps in the corridor
as nurses talk to each other
and go about their work.

Unable to move, I listen
to sounds that rarely become
distinct words – fragments
that are human, and comforting.

Old men in Ward 7

An illusion of effigies
broken when one groans
or another cries out.

One talks to himself,
mazed among faces and times,
once and always the child
calling his parents
who have moved out of reach.

I listen unwillingly, visualising
each in his bed, as I am,
not a statue, but a man
of spirit and living flesh,
who longs for sleep, and hopes,
when dawn comes, to wake.

Elwin

Old man with white hair
singing to himself
who might be my father
towards the end.

Elwin – his voice soft
and sweet, but faltering,
a resonance of other times
with his male voice choir,
a memory of communal song.

Clouds at Evening

Slow moving
            shape shifting
bringing colour to a grey day
as they drift along the ridge

            wanderers
            wayfarers

clouds that are dreams
on the mind's ocean

figures on a journey
whose destination
we should know
            but cannot guess

Wanting sleep

Not death, but
the kind dark
mind a pool
with no tremor
an empty stage
for the play in which you act
all the parts, or none
and the name of the play,
you wish, is Peace.

Solstice

Sleepless, through a night
never quite dark,
my mind overworks
releasing image after image.

They are migrants
flying in from some place
that is deep in time,
drawn here by a power
that I seem to possess
but do not understand.

Do I make these images,
or am I the being
that these images make?

Midsummer dawn:
the sun over the ridge
a fiery eye, sky sharp as cut stone.
As I turn from the light burning through glass
word after word departs
leaving me empty
with an aching skull.

View from Ward 7

Light moves along the ridge
catching the blades
of a wind turbine, illuminating
white houses of the new town.

Looking out,
I imagine the air brushing my face
and think of old Merthyr,
the town my great-grandfather
may have known, with its hovels
for the sick and poor,
filthy alleys and cholera graves,
and the energy driving through
that powered an empire.

As I look out, imagining
fresh air touching my face,
it is easy to think of them,
the shadowy generations
but not to understand the life
of each man, woman and child.

Turning from the window,
I resume the routine of a new day
as nurses bring us comfort
and medicated ease.

In and out of the ward

On the TV in the corner
the public world is a play
of clowns jostling
for power and position.
Unbelievable words are spoken.

In the ward, nurses
move quietly, efficiently,
bringing kindness, and,
where needed, humour to every bed.

Is that the world
in the corner, the real world
or a nightmare from which we cannot wake?

Mighty men, great women,
leaders who would be,
mouths that are full of promises.

Words & smiles & boasts,
mouths & mouths.

The TV is switched off
closing on the last mouth
as it opens, big with promise.

Unobtrusively
nurses come and go
in the dimmed light.

Escape

Over the hills
     as a shadow chases cloud
     as a clod springing up
      becomes lark
as thought from the lamed body
      flies
beyond the blinds
as word leaps to lips
seeking a way
      over the hills

Kuzula

I believe in angels
because I've met one –
            Kuzula,
a small black woman
from Zambia,
not a wing in sight,
who came to me
in the night hours,
telling me truths
with a hard realism
kindly, as only an angel can.

Baby and Mother

Baby with dreaming eyes
on her mother's shoulder,
thumb in mouth,
who seems to look at me,
what does she see?

Nothing yet, perhaps.
But how can nothing be?

Her mother smiles,
the baby smiles,
as if sharing a secret
no one else will ever know.

Symphony

For Seán Street

1
Listening, I hear
 stone becoming music
from crypt to pinnacle –
        gargoyle mouthings
        bell voice
sounding the depth of time
fluting
            fluttering
                        trilling
of little birds
on sonorous branches
and over all
and through all
tides of human song
filling the airy nave.

2
In minutes the building
laboured into place
stone on stone
through centuries
becomes a cathedral of sound.

3
I put my headphones down,
returning immediately
to this mortal house
of flesh, where a man
who does not know where he is
shouts with pain
and trollies grind
on corridor floors.
Lights brighten and dim

on steel instruments
and plastic tubes
in the long, dark hours
and nurses
bring medication
and a friendly word
to the sleepless
and prayerful sick.

Antithesis

Evening sun through blinds
and on roofs of cars
in the hospital carpark.
Through my earplugs
a concert from Snape Maltings,
some lovely fragments.
                    In the corridor
a woman screams
and is hushed gently
by nurses, but screams
and screams again.
                    In the bed opposite
an old man with thin legs
lies among bed sheets
and pillows like an ancient child.

A cry, the sound
of a zimmer grating on the floor,
outside a workman shouting to his mate
and in my head the music
of a distant world.

Conversation

for Philip Gross

Lights dimmed, the ward
prepares for sleep.
I lie awake, listening
through headphones
to a late programme:
a discussion between poets
of the word 'common'.

Out of the air,
                    a voice I recognise.

Quaker friend,
what inner light shines
for our souls' dark?
In this ward, we are
castaways, each adrift.
The sea restive, endless.

I hear you, speaking
with quick intelligence,
exchanging ideas
in some bright room.
For you, poetry is conversation –
voice speaks to voice
now, and across the ages

It is the truth I wish for,
in this place, where
the tide of sleep laps
each man thrown up
on the strand of self,
alone in his private dark.

Seagull

Flash of a white wing
as a gull turns past
the hospital window
and takes my mind with it,
leaving town and fly-tipped moors
to follow the Taff to the sea.

Love- messenger,
you fly from this moment
into another time, when
two figures walk hand in hand
on shingle between estuary
and sea, and the salt air
and the sun sparkling on small waves
as they break, and the sound of feet
crunching pebbles and shells,
and the lighthouse on white rocks
in the blue sea, and the yachts
with red and yellow sails –
all of it, the whole world
present to sense and sight –
this moment
and all the days that will come
without end, are simply a gift.

Constable cloud study

I open the book
and the painting
reveals itself.
                    Suddenly
the ceiling over my head
vanishes. Cloud
unbound pours into sight.
It might be streaming
over the planet's rim –
a maelstrom, in which
three buzzards wheel,
tiny in such space
yet somehow defining it,
                    storm-riders
wings stretched
for the currents of air,
denizens of the quick world
which, startled for a moment,
breaks me from the cocoon
of the ward, and releases
in me a shout of joy.

Home

The light has changed,
as you would always observe.
At the edge of sight, a leaf
or butterfly flutters down
from birches in the quarry wood.

Indoors, the familiar returns
with a rush – paintings, books,
sculptures, the living space
we shared and you still animate.

Settling in, I recall
fragments of the past weeks –
voices in corridors,
footsteps in the dark.

I think of Elwin
who crossed the ward
to shake hands, apologising
for disturbing the night
with cries and groans.

I remember him singing
to himself, softly
with faltering harmony
as he called back a time
once shared, that had gone
but was still alive in his voice.

4.

Diary 26 April–28 May 2020

26 April

Following blood tests and days of increasing weakness, I'm now back in Prince Charles hospital due to my impaired kidneys. Paramedics Rachel & Russell, former PC & miner, brought me in. Good, warm people. It is evening and I'm in Ward 2 again. Before the ambulance arrived, I just had time to complete reading the proofs of *Art of Seeing* and send them to Tony Frazer. This has been a period of weeks I wouldn't have got through without Joe.

Placed in a bed next to Bryn. We recognise each other and exchange friendly, old man, greetings.

27 April

Clear explanation from a doctor of my damaged kidneys and the treatment needed to help them function. A blood transfusion in the night continues this morning. I lie in bed, read, think, turn over my 'Welsh' book, beginning with Aberystwyth & Carol, in my mind.

Dim view through blinds of hospital buildings & part of Merthyr. Covid cases are, of course, in another ward. I'm told the problem is not severe here. Nurse Jo, from Ebbw Vale, helps me out of bed and to wash. Old familiarity returns.

After lunch: ultra sound for kidneys & testicles. Pushed in trolley by Jeff, former colliery worker, as many auxiliary staff are.

29 April

Awake at 4 feeling low. Steadied by reading *Horizon*. Cloudy day, end, perhaps, of this most beautiful April, when nature has been left largely to itself. Short walk with physios & zimmer. Fourth 'start' in more than 20 years.

30 April

With oxygen & on a drip, I wait for urologist & kidney specialist. Bryn, who is poorly, is taken home. We wish each other well. John, across the room, is my only neighbour now. He had an accident at home, lying trapped for hours, and damaging his leg. Lee rings first while urologist & assistant struggle unsuccessfully to fit a catheter. I continue story of Carol's introduction to Wales.

Afternoon. On bed. Calls from Bethan, Lee, Joe, Adele. Resting, or reading *Horizon*, and Cottingham's *In Search of the Soul*. Watching cloud crossing blue sky, one big cloud like a barrage balloon. A sense out there of driving power, in here, of quiet efficiency & care. It shakes me sometimes to think how disabled I am, though not feeling troubled in myself. John is being removed to Mountain Ash. For now, I shall be alone in this ward. From this window, I now realise, from talking to a male nurse, the hill I can see is the near side of the open-cast mine at Fochriw, on the moorland, from which the distant Beacons and Black Mountains can be seen.

Joined by Roy. Fragments of a life story across the room. Shaken to find that with retention of water I weigh 20 stone. I feel the weight, the burden of flesh.

1 May

Bright sun in cloudy sky. Walk across room with physios. Doctor cheers me by telling me I have lost more than 2 kilos, so the diuretic drip is having effect. Dr Taylor talks to me about the option of dialysis, which sounds terrible.

I look out of the window at the clouds changing shape, moving over, slow but never still, and the blue sky between and behind, and have a sense of the wonder of this planet, the world made for life, and made *by* life. The building where I am being cared for is house of the burden of flesh, but also of tenderness, and care, and consideration for all. I have been seen by numerous doctors, specialists, and nurses, and although my future is unclear, I begin to feel that I may live, that this will be an episode, not yet the end. And what I feel is the wonder of life, whose precariousness I know.

Messages from Adele, Debbie, Liz Mathews. Attempt poem on Cottingham in search of the soul.

2 May

New neighbour, possibly suffering from dementia, makes a lot of noise in the night, repeating letters over and over, until Roy shouts at him.

Morning. Cheery nurse from Tredegar gives me my pills. We talk about Tredegar, and about Mark Williams, local boy & snooker champion. I mention Chris Meredith, novelist and poet from Tredegar.

Window open slightly brings me a little breeze. Sun shining.

'Small world': Amy & Roy swop family connections. I meet nurse Jim again, and lovely L.

'To myself I am but darkness.'
Nicolas Malebranche

"Man really exists as man only when he uses the word 'God' at least as a question."
Karl Rahner
(Both quoted in John Cottingham, *In Search of the Soul*)

3 May

After breakfast, call from Philip Gross before he goes on line to a Quaker meeting. We agree that after the 'pest' we will need to live with common sense. He demurs at my word 'purify', which I realise has malign political associations. Ironically, the natural world is purer for our diminished 'footprints' (e.g. air & road traffic, pressure on countryside).

Roy finds another nurse with whom he shares place & family associations. I partially overhear their excited talk, and begin to feel, for the first time here, an outsider, which makes me feel melancholy, and even a spasm of anger. (I've spent a large part of my life helping to educate young Welsh men & women, but remain an alien presence in Wales.)

Calls from Joe & Emily, Adele, Bernard, Julie Pritchard (who's heard 4 cuckoos in her walks). Cats, a young doctor, talks to me clearly. She has 'no crystal ball' but surmises that I will be back in hospital periodically for drip treatment to help my kidneys get rid of liquid. At present, this is working well. After sleeping badly last night, I have had a lazy day mainly in bed, and writing and reading. The sketch of my Welsh memoir is more or less complete. Of course, life escapes.

4 May

Good sleep. Bright morning. Sophy weighs me: 18.2 stone after 20 stone the other day. She's very upfront, calls me 'posh'. We chat happily. Annette & Helen give me a shower, then Annette, formerly a hairdresser, cuts my beard. Back in bed, refreshed. Dr Taylor tells me I have a lot more liquid to shed and will be in for another week or two.

After lunch, Joe rings me, stressed. Then a long talk with Chris. Walk with physio across room. Nurse asks me what I'm writing. 3rd call from Joe, who reads me a loving letter from my brother Tony, which begins, of course, with a denunciation of Prince Charles 'running round in a military uniform'.

Reading Cottingham's highly rational book in search of the soul, I realise that what I am always hoping for is to be persuaded of the immortality of the soul – survival of the beloved person. This has troubled me life-long – more so since deaths of those I love. Some higher idea of the self's ability to espouse goodness is not what I seek. St Paul's 'spiritual body' is more to the point. Resurrection à la Stanley Spencer speaks to the child in me. What I don't want is wishful thinking. If the truth is final death, let me try to face it. Until we die, love does not end.

Evening. Dark outside. I now share this room with one other man, in the bed opposite. I wonder if L. will be on the ward tonight. I am attracted to this sympathetic woman. At the same time, I caution myself.

5 May

Card from Adele. Dr Taylor pleased, and perhaps rather surprised, by my rate of liquid loss.

Reassuring talks with diabetic nurse & social services. Long talk with Kay. David Lloyd rings from America. Norman tells me Deborah's novel is to be filmed.

6 May

Bright, breezy. Little sleep due to itching. Chloe, from Rhymney, helps me out of bed. 21 years old. I tell her about our Chloe, my granddaughter. I sit on my chair, in a breeze. Now in this room with three other old men I feel quite the youth – which just means I'm more alert and don't look – or feel – that I'm dying.

Nurses tell me that I have 'the prize for weight loss today' – down to 16+ stone. Sun on white roofs of Merthyr, visible through blinds. Evening of a lovely day, quiet in this room. Phlebotomist got blood out of me at second attempt. Finished Barry Lopez's *Horizon*: a wide-ranging book in space and time, full of beauty and horror. Sexual desire begins to return.

Evening. Long talk with Emily, who rings up very distressed over her impending divorce. Em. takes after her grandmother, Ivy, and we are remaking the relationship we should have had when I left to live in the Netherlands, when she was a little girl. We *are* remaking this, which is wonderful for both of us. She feels much better as we talk. But I caution her – she knows this really – grieving continues. It doesn't just stop.

7 May

17 stone. Walking good enough, so physio signs me off. After lunch I slept until 4, when Andrea woke me up and got me out of bed for supper. After dark: two nurses at the window. What are you looking at? A big orange full moon rising from behind the hill above Merthyr. What does it mean? I mumble something about weather & season.

8 May

With weight loss, nurses comment on how different I look.

Mieke's birthday: 74. Not always a good day: she would subvert special occasions by drinking.

V.E. Day. I remember the trestle table in Greenaway Lane, the party, fireworks. 75 years ago. I recall my small number of wartime memories. My parents ensured that I had a happy childhood.

Calls from Bethan & Elin for Mieke's birthday. Listened to a radio programme of Horatio Clare walking Offa's Dyke with contributions from Chris Meredith in Welsh and in English. As a Welsh learner, Chris took himself deeper into his area of Wales, as can be heard in his voice, and seen in the range and depth of his novels and poems. Joe brings me in books & papers and leaves them with a nurse who brings them up to me.

We are part of nature, but nature is so much more than we can know, even in a ditch or hedgerow. We hear birds singing, but so much more is going on. We sense the life stream but all that composes it escapes us. Listen, don't try to analyse.

'The first great intense shared experience since the Second World War.' (Lord Peter Hennessy, speaking positively about the hoped-for effect of the virus.)

'One can only love one's country with a broken heart.'
(Frank-Walter Steinmeier, President of Germany)

He was speaking of Germany, but isn't this true for all of us if we recognise the crimes of Empire?

9 May

Woke feeling heavy from dream of being lost and driving endlessly through country. Shower. Joe rings and tells me Tony Frazer has done the cover of my *Selected Poems* with an image of my father's painting, *The Road to Keyhaven*. Then a good long talk with Colin Edwards, who had seen the first swallows in this bird-friendly air.

10 May

Heavy external atmosphere making me feel sluggish. Good talk with Chris after lunch. Emily, feeling flat: divorce on Tuesday.

Young doctor, Jemima, sympathetic and very direct. The treatment hasn't been working well today. If it fails, my only choice will be dialysis. Dr Taylor scared me at the prospect. But if it is the only way I can live, so be it. It may not come to this; the days ahead will tell.

Evening. Anthony Nanson rings. He has finished indexing *Art of Seeing*. We talk about George Seferis. Anthony recommends Roderick Beaton's biography.

Dramatization on Radio 4 of Keith Douglas, based on the poet's words. Brave man, good poet.

11 May

The man across the ward asks whether they come round with newspapers. Not during lockdown, I tell him. 'I'm going to be bored bloody rigid today.' So far, boredom hasn't been my problem, but uncertain outcome/ diagnosis makes me restive. (I confess to never having had, in the sense of deeply felt, what George Oppen in *Discrete Series* refers to as 'The knowledge… of boredom'.)

The man in the bed beside me is a troubling presence. He is confused, often out of bed, looking for a phone which nurses tell him he has left at home. He disturbs the usually peaceful ward.

Calls from Joe, Adele. I read (Weber's *The Biology of* Wonder), draft a poem, 'The Widower'.

12 May

My disturbing neighbour made a lot of noise last night. Nurse Chloe engages the old man across the room, encouraging him to eat and talk, but mostly he stares blankly into space. Joe rings, very agitated at the prospect of being unprepared when I'm sent home. He rings again later to say sorry.

Before supper, while nurses are struggling to get a cannula into me (for penicillin to treat an infection caused by another cannula) a card arrives from Sue. Almost immediately, she phones to tell me about an Antiques Road Show from Southampton Water, shortly on TV. Alone in old age, this is how memory returns, as I felt it would years ago. One can change/remake one's life, but one can't unmake a shared past.

Breakfast. Jim talks to me about his poetry. He knows about Mike Jenkins & readings at The Imp in Merthyr. Amy, from Tredegar, tells me how different I look with weight loss. Very encouraging.

Finished Andreas Weber's *The Biology of Wonder*. An inspiring book about 'poetic ecology', one that makes us *feel* the world we are. Weber calls Rilke's *Weltinnenraum*, 'interior space of the world', or 'world inscape', linking Rilke and Gerard Manley Hopkins. 'This space is the realm of poetry, but also of *poiesis*, of creation. They are all connected by the *conditio vital*, which is shared by everything alive.' Weber is a forthright thinker who has no hesitation in replacing conventional biology with his biology of feeling & subjectivity. He is unfair to Darwin, as David Abram notes.

Call from Diana Wallace who is in the thick of marking student scripts. My neighbour is shouting for some reason in a loud unreasonable voice.

Late afternoon. Séan Street rings. Coincidentally, (since I hope to offer a piece on his work to *Agenda*), just after I've read, in the latest *Agenda*, Michael Alexander on a meeting with Ezra Pound in old age. 'In the depression and perhaps remorse of his last decades he often expressed profound doubts as to whether his work had any value.' David Jones expressed such doubts about his own work to me. Christopher Middleton, too. And doubts were always there with R. S. Thomas. This will be the way in a culture that does not value its poets, at least the more demanding ones. (In England, the more modernist.) Why was it different with T. S. Eliot? Because of his *critical* eminence & power base at Faber. Because *The Waste Land* had defined an age. Because his later work, especially the plays, was far less challenging. Yet I suspect that Pound the poet remains most enlivening for other poets.

14 May

Uncomfortable night due to slight indigestion & a light that wouldn't turn off. Dr Nolan visits in the morning. We recognise each other from last year. She says, tentatively, I may go home next week as out-patient. Two nice young women phlebotomists get blood out of me with difficulty. A cannula, put in after a struggle, had to be taken out when the drip hurt me.

15 May

Could eat little supper because of indigestion. Calls so far today from Joe, Norman, Adele, Elin. Liz tells Joe Frances has the Covid virus, in spite of all their precautions. Ivor, across the room from me, sits in his chair looking in my direction. He was found wandering outside his home in Brecon. I wonder if the dog roses are out in the garden at home. I missed the celandines this year, and so much more.

16 May

Beginning of another hospital weekend. May it be my last before going home.

Reading Sarah Gridley's *Insofar*, the collection of poems she has kindly dedicated to me, with an epigraph from my 'As a thousand years'. She is a poet of consistent authority, her very tentativeness and indeterminacy distinctively voiced. She works from the word as a unit, questioning meanings, and from sensations of a material, relational world – bird, trees, fire, water – relishing 'the stark apostles, wind, snow, and stone// … what is/seasonal and real'. Her passages of vivid sensory perception aren't ends in themselves. Forrest Gander says she 'inaugurates the school of existential intimacy'. 'Intimacy' nicely catches the quality of subjectivity revealed here – the sense of poetic alchemy, with matter fluid, transformative, as Sarah writes: 'I wish for things/in addition to water//to take on/the shimmer of water'. Her poems often baffle the mind seeking a specific hold – a what, a where – but their attention requires the reader's attention. How refreshing compared to the poetry of egotistic subjectivity, photographic in details of the poet's experience.

Sarah's poems quicken my mind and make me think of possibilities of lyric poetry – various as poets with inwardness (always in relation to outward reality). Otherwise a flat day, in which I sit or lie down, relieved that, because it is Saturday, no one comes to take blood. With deep, narrow veins, I am a difficult subject, so my arms are full of needle pricks. Cloud covers part of Merthyr I can see through the window. The hill ridge behind calls to me.

A nurse, Matthew, who sees me writing, asks me about it, as nurses and doctors sometimes do. In reply, I mention – quickly – that I write poetry. It embarrasses me to do so; though some people show interest, it sets me apart. I have got better in this respect. Once, in similar circumstances, I would have kept quiet. Yet, there's a sort of snobbery in this denial, which assumes people won't understand. With modern poetry, a fair assumption. But one has to trust the person who asks, and to trust oneself with an answer.

17 May

Shower, helped by Chloe, from Rhymney. I mention Idris Davies to her. She hasn't heard of the poet but tells me there's an Idris Davies school in Rhymney. I remember the river Rhymney running past our garden in Machen – how long ago it seems since M., and I came to live in South Wales. Here, I'm learning patience with my strange, talkative new neighbour, who is in pain, and making noises, as well as giggling and singing. Monologic 'conversation' – much of which I fail to understand. How intensely we live inside ourselves! I write about the poem as objectifying the personal. Is that what I do? Does making also inevitably mean making *up*? Self-knowledge is a fine thing. But how can we ever be sure we have it? We are such partial beings in our self-understanding. Only God knows us, as Gerard said.

Good talk with Chris after lunch. My disturbed neighbour has been raging loudly most of today. Uttering threats against certain persons. Nurses have tried to quieten him, without success. Phone call from Gavin Edwards, now living in London. We talk about Brueghel & Bosch, and Dickens, subject of his forthcoming book. Gavin is a kind man. The old department at Glamorgan was marked by kindness.

Tried in the evening to listen to a radio production of Louis MacNeice's *The Dark Tower*, but my neighbour's noise prevented me from hearing it. He is a sick man, dying (he says), and mentally ill, a fantasist who calls on the support of celebrities he claims to be related to, who will take revenge on those ill-treating him. His noise & antics strain my patience and teach me charity.

18 May

Another night disturbed by my neighbour's noise. Dr Nolan tells me I may be able to go home on Thursday. No one can predict the future, but my kidney function may be stabilized by medication. For how long? Deterioration will ensue – and dialysis? For now, with weight loss, I feel pretty good. But how provisional life is! Work while the day lasts.

This morning I've been fiddling with a draft of 'In praise of windows' (for Liz Mathews). There's a moment – word, image, phrase – when a poem 'takes off', before which it's flat, dead on the page. It's as if there's an animating spirit – an aliveness – that comes, or doesn't come. *Overwork* prevents it, as if the mind were a muscle that becomes taut, stressed. There are gifts, but work is usually necessary. Then, *relax.*

19 May

Morning begins with my neighbour's loud voice, and a call from Social Services arranging meals-on-wheels for me, from this Friday. I'm sure Mother used to deliver meals-on-wheels in Pennington. How time changes our situations, as life ceases to be the stream we scarcely think of, and becomes a struggle to make it flow. We remember the past in old age because we *see* experiences once lived, not seen at the time, but participated in. 'Careless' was once the word, as John Constable knew, when he spoke of his boyhood beside the River Stour.

Jodie, from Merthyr, gives me a bath which is very refreshing. She too calls me 'posh' because of my accent. A call from Sandy Arnold after lunch. We talk about Arnolds Wood which is now being looked after by Bradford-upon-Avon borough council. I remember the day in February when we planted the trees in memory of Les, and the time before my stroke, at Leigh House Farm, and looking with M. for a house in the area. A nurse comes to take a swab. A patient in another ward has been found to have the Covid virus. How lucky we are in this age, when you think how it must have been in times of plague, before modern medicine. But how bewildered many of us are with our normal lives taken away. In premodern times we would have been trying desperately to appease God, and flagellating ourselves and each other, as monks did in Winchester in the Middle Ages.

Talk with Séan who tells me about his 5-year-old granddaughter's love of poetry. I remember my time with schoolchildren in Fareham, when I realized children experience the animate universe and are natural poets. My neighbour, bored, turns up the TV in the ward very loud and dances in front of it to popular music. He then tells part of his fantastic life story to a new patient, Neville, who has replaced Ivor in the bed opposite me.

20 May

Dazzling sun. A nurse tells me this will be the hottest day of the year so far. We need rain. After flood, drought. After complacency, virus.

Diana Wallace sends me a lovely card, David Jones, *A Ship off Ynys Byr*. He was a painter who embraced the world he loved. This also is the meaning of his shapes that 'contain' images of the Christian universe. I sketch a poem for Diana based on the painting. Dr Nolan tells me it is 99 per cent certain that I'll go home tomorrow.

Drama after lunch: my neighbour shouting, raging, issuing threats against security men & nurses. Occasioned, I think, by his anger with the mental health team and their plans for him. Neville, who speaks with difficulty, told him to grow up. I held my peace. He has a huge sense of grievance and speaks with a voice full of self-pity. I too came close to shouting – which would have made things worse. At times, he sounded like the impotent King Lear, who would do 'such things' to his enemies! Nurses and doctors reacted with patience.

28 May

I came out of hospital a week ago, returning to find bunches of small green berries on the rowan, where there had been white blossoms when I was taken in. Outdoors, I can still hear the birdsong, which will have been louder in recent weeks. I'm about as mobile as I was before this illness, and will have to watch my weight. Joe has brought down a garden seat, where I should be able to sit and look out across the valley. Like old men I remember in Northover Road, when I was a boy! But my mind is still active in reading and writing. I hope now to be able to add a section to 'The Release'.

5.

Widower

He has gone walkabout
in the dim-lit hours,
peering in faces
of fellow patients
who are asleep, or wander
in landscapes of their own.
He alone is awake, crossing
the outback of a dream,
cast out to wander, peering
in each face for one face,
listening for the voice
that will tell him who he is.

On a painting by David Jones
for Diana Wallace

The arms of the bay
enclose a little ship
with an orange funnel,
smoke streaming aft.
On the cliff, a tiny tree
shows the blast of the wind.
Think of him standing
behind a window,
steadied by what he sees,
this man who makes a shape
of a world created whole
which he remembers torn apart.

In Praise of Windows

for Liz Mathews

1
Look – it begins with dawn,
this apparition
which gradually becomes
a world without walls –
trees, and birds in the trees,
clouds, mountains of cloud,
and all for the gift of glass
that lets the outside enter
and the inside reach out.

2
I begin this in hospital,
hoping, Liz, to respond
to your challenge – someone,
you said, should write a poem
in praise of windows.
So why not me?

3
Think of them, patients,
prisoners, all who are confined:
what a little glass means,
an eye for the eye
to receive light,
as I do here, through
blinds, watching
this apparition
which gradually becomes
a world without walls,
cloud moving along the hills
and a seagull, white in the sun.

Truly, we owe thanks
to the art of the glazier
which lets the outside enter
and the inside reach out
driving back the dark

A philosopher in search of the soul

1
H sits in his study, books
and computer on his desk, while
Plato's chariot races through his mind.

Dark horse, light horse –
                                                    how they scatter
thought – a tumult of reason
and desire, which, momentarily,
Aristotle calms, restoring soul
to the body's shape.

Now old Yeats disturbs his calm.
What am I, he thinks, if not
                                        a paltry thing,
a scarecrow with a tattered book,
or as the learned fool has said,
a piece of cosmic scum?

2
Head on the desk, he sleeps,
and dreams a Cookham dream
of tombs prized open
where the new-hatched dead
rise up, dazed with surprise.
They shake off dust, and climbing
to the light, resume their lives.

3
He wakes to thoughts
of parents, lover, friends –
a cloud in which each face appears.
Do they dissolve, from being
into nothingness?
A whisper in his ear:

To philosophise
is to learn to die.
A sudden wind storms
through the room,
tearing pages from his books.
He is alone, his study scattered
to the elements – a man exposed
upon an inner shore,
that fronts an outer tide.

4
Grief is the sea
that sends a shockwave to his heart.
     Where is the life
that I saw die from the beloved eyes?
                    Gone,
for ever gone,
Anima, breath of life,
                    no word
can tell me what I seek,
no image and no shade.
What lasts is memory,
which is an inner sea, now
calm, now storming at the walls of sense
but never still until I die.

6.

Diary 9 July–7 August 2020

9 July

Back in hospital after a period of increasing heaviness & debility. In familiar Ward 2, my home from home. Greeted by nurses and by Dr Nolan. Listening to Test Match cricket on the radio. Reading Wilson Knight's *The Starlit Dome*. Knight was a *reader*, but so detailed that he makes Wordsworth seem a bore, which, over stretches of verse, perhaps he was. Knight describes 'the Wordsworthian profundity' in 'the interactions of the temporal and the eternal'. His description of Wordsworth as 'a Norse poet, happiest in bleak solitudes, for whom we must go to Old English poetry, The Wanderer and The Seafarer for a parallel' is especially suggestive.

10 July

Bright morning. Bath. Visit from Dr Karen Hamilton who speaks positively of my weight loss. Still unable to stand without assistance. Thinking about poems, 'Archie' & 'Nurse', intuition returning with imaginative/verbal energy. *The Starlit Dome* makes me impatient with Coleridge's interminable idealising. What I long for is language of the real, as in Clare, actual fields & working landscape, real dirt, not 'flowery' words. Of course, history has exposed the idealising mind, which couldn't survive mechanical warfare, industrialization, scepticism. Religious belief has to be tougher than that. As Coleridge's, in his suffering, was.

12 July

Feeling heavy after night without much sleep, though I tend to sleep in the afternoon. Message from Bethan on holiday in Bulgaria. Call from Peter Larkin to thank me for my books, which Tony Frazer has sent him. Peter is in touch with Robert Baker, whose book on George Oppen and René Char, *In Dark Again in Wonder*, we both admire. I made contact for him through Sarah Gridley. I lie in bed, reading, listening to cricket on the radio, or just lying. I have ideas for poems, but lack creative energy. Ideas alone don't make poems.

13 July

Felt sick after lunch yesterday. High temperature this morning. Wheeled downstairs for ultra sound for kidneys. Washed and feeling better after morning porridge & tea. Back from ultra sound, sketched a poem for Archie.

15 July

Better night after a bad day, appetite returning. Poems working in my mind: 'Archie', 'Nurses', 'White Horse Hill'. I'm glad to be near the end of *The Starlit Dome*. Shelley's flights on angel-pilot weary me. By contrast, I love Keats's earthiness, which resists abstraction. Today, Wilson Knight's connection between literature and Spiritualism is so unfashionable as not to be seen or understood, and if seen, derided. But for me it breathes fresher air than materialistic deconstruction and its derivatives. My reservation is less about truths Knight reveals, than about the tendency of all to be One Truth.

In the afternoon, long, exhausting talk on the phone with a Broker, preparatory to releasing money from our house to allow Emily to keep hers.

16 July

Another night without sleep, poems & essays from my new books filling my mind. After breakfast, while having my blood pressure taken, I catch myself boasting to a nurse about all the books I have written.

Refreshing bath. Back to bed.

Afternoon. Exhausted. Unable to get out of bed for physio. Talks with Joe, and with Philip, who is working online to save the Woodbrooke Quaker centre.

'...only one attribute separates humans from superorganisms like those of ants, wasps, or termites: hominids never totally give up the defence of their individuality for the interests of the hive or, in our case, the community.' (Edward O Wilson)

Jean Earle made the same point in a poem.

Andre, across the room from me, is Polish. He understands little English, and must feel isolated.

Long talks with Chris who, when I told him I was raising equity from our house, offered to lend me money. What a friend he is. I can, however, manage from my own resources.

17 July

L. appeared on the ward last night: warm & friendly. I slept better but woke from a dream in which I committed a terrible crime and was being hunted down. I've had similar dreams quite often but wouldn't call them nightmares compared to some I experienced as a boy. I wake thoughtful, not shaking.

Weight loss continues. Out of bed, in my chair, standing with minimal help. Two enlivening phone-calls. First, Colin, who tells me the interview he conducted with me is on the Wales Arts Review website. Next, Adele, who is reading a book about Coleridge's wife, so we have a long talk about S.T.C. & the Wordsworths.

18 July

Too little sleep at night. Anxiety dreams in the early morning. But better generally.

Dear Norman Schwenk rings after lunch on his 85th birthday. He is doing well since his illness 3 or 4 years ago. Filming of Deborah's novel has been postponed due to the Covid virus. But they've received the money upfront!

Waking up, I sometimes have the frightening sensation of seeing a strange person, gone in a flash. My rational mind tells me this is generated by some object in the room. But it is a haunting experience. Mieke and I used to promise not to haunt each other, in the event of dying first. I wish sometimes she would appear, though I feel her invisible presence, and she is rarely far from my mind.

So far, all the scientists I have read in the book of interviews (*Mind, Life, and Universe*) assume that the mind is the brain. Perhaps it is. So why should the fact (if that is what it is) depress me? Because it reduces 'spirit' to an entirely physical phenomenon. We humans remain mysterious, but science (in the estimation of some scientists, at least) moves towards explaining everything.

My two neighbours, in beds by the window, are elderly, tubby South Walians who call each other 'Butt'. Overhearing them, I wonder what I'm doing here, in this country that is so foreign to the English. It is evening now, and dark outside. We all lie on our beds, asleep, or thinking our thoughts. And we call this 'one world'!

20 July

When the curtains were drawn this morning the sun blinded me.

Joe's birthday. Things seem to be good for him at present. He has been very active, tidying the house and working in the garden. Tomorrow he will be with his son preparing to bring Harry back to spend some time with us.

A better day after a bad night due to pain in my leg. I worried that this might be something life-threatening, such as a blood clot, but a doctor tells me the pain is caused by lying in bed too long. A shower refreshes me but I'm tired.

21 July

Some walking this morning. A doctor tells me I'm being transferred to the renal unit at The University Hospital of Wales, known as The Heath, in Cardiff.

22 July

One small step forward: walking to the bathroom to wash myself.

The interviews with scientists in *Mind, Life, and the Universe* become fascinating. I find discussions of the bacterial origins of life especially interesting.

'We humans are one very recent blink, only a sparkle in the eye of evolution of a persistent, sturdy, powerful, single huge life-form on planet Earth.' (Ricardo Guerrero)

'The first hominid (*Australopithecus afarensis*) dates back more than two million years. Fragile and petite with a cranial capacity only one-third of that of her descendants, Lucy was already a person from head to toe.' (Eduardo Punset)

I wonder if Wordsworth was in the mind of whoever named this 'first hominid'.

'Science is the only news,' according to Lynn Margulis. Yet, she loved the poetry of Emily Dickinson, which brings us news each time we read it.

23 July

Transferred by ambulance to The Heath. Lovely breeze outside the hospital, and now a room with a view! Towards Penarth and the Bay. A strip of water, a line of hills.

A doctor, Don, visits my bed and starts the conversation about dialysis. Alan, in the bed opposite, who is experienced with dialysis, reassures me. Peter, on the machine, is in some pain or discomfort. I shall be in here for at least another week. I feared it would come to this: dialysis or death. Now dialysis is coming, I feel more positive.

24 July

Good night's sleep after doctor gave me a sleeping pill. First day at The Heath, mostly in bed, and quite comfortable. Refreshing to see sky through wide windows without blinds.

25 July

Wind got up in the night, Gulls cried outside the tall building. Sleepless, I listened.

Alone in the ward, I work on 'Archie', 'Nurses', and 'White Horse Hill'.

26 July

Sunday morning. After breakfast, I drafted a new version of 'The Bridge'. This was the subject of my first published poem, beyond school magazines & *Second Wessex*, in *Universities Poetry*. It meant so much to me, that place where, in a magical hour, I caught my first little trout. I could walk there in my mind now, from Hayford, down Hazel Road, on the lane through Wainsford Common – unless, a few years later, I met J. on the way, and we lay by a field gate making love.

Drafted 'Gulls'.

Afternoon. Talk with Séan who is proposing to write a book about ways in which writers, e.g., Hardy, Jefferies, and Edward Thomas, convey a sense of sound with the written word. He and Joanne now live not far from Liverpool Airport. They noted the clamour of birds, once planes started flying again. Joanne speculated that this was due to the alarm of birds fledged this year, that had never heard an airplane.

Listening to a programme of jazz requests on radio takes me back to weekly sessions at the Yellow Dog jazz club in Bevois Valley, Southampton, when I was a student. Smoky, crowded room, bodies jostling & the thrill of Trad Jazz, which was our thing when we were young. Of course, it meant sex too, or lack of sex. I have loved deeply over the years, but for the intensity of bitter-sweet romantic young love I remember dancing with J. in the front room of her council house at Pennington Oval. Clumsy youth that I was! Heart-smitten.

27 July

Woke at 9. 30 last night thinking it was morning. Shower. Working on 'What is poetry for?' It is the question that has haunted modern poets, at least, since Hölderlin.

I feel this poem, if it is to come to anything, will have to wait until later, perhaps a lot later, if I live so long. I wonder, though, would it be too simple to say that every real poem, every poem that rings true, is the implicit answer to this question?

Talks with Chris, and with Séan, with whom I recall David Gascoyne on our visits to the Isle of Wight, and in Winchester, when I'd invited him to speak to students at the School of Art. We remember David and Judy, the story of their extraordinary meeting, and how charming David could be, or, at times, silent and beyond communication.

28 July

After days of anxiety, even fear, imagining dialysis, I learnt today that

I might not need it – now, anyway. If all goes well, I could be at home by the weekend, or soon after. Reading Tim Blanchard's *Powysland,* an attractively personal 'discovery' of John Cowper Powys. Why this metropolitan hostility to Powys, this history of ignorant dismissal? It can't be only because his Romances are so long! I think it's because J.C.P. calls into question what passes for seriousness among English literati. Our home-grown geniuses, such as Blake, Stanley Spencer, and Powys, have a kind of naïve earnestness, and they are visionary, without irony, and celebrate parochial or local life – Weymouth, Peckham, Cookham. Supremely intelligent, they're not clever.

29 July

I learnt this morning that I may be able to go home later this week, and return later to have a fistula fitted, so that I can receive dialysis.
The other book I'm reading is *The Magic Mountain.* Actually, rereading, since I first read it at Vicky's instigation many years ago, when I was a postgraduate. I went on to read a lot of Thomas Mann at that time, but knew there was much in *The Magic Mountain* I had to return to. A book to read in an institution, perhaps!

A lazy day for me in bed, dozing, reading. The man in the bed beside me is obviously very ill. His wife & daughter have been allowed in to sit with him, in spite of the lockdown. Bethan and Agnes rang from the Netherlands. Séan has written a poem for me after our conversation yesterday. Joe read it to me over the phone.

30 July

Bright morning. Refreshing shower, with Virgil, originally from South Africa. Talking about his name, he cited *Thunderbirds,* and was pleased when I mentioned the great Roman poet. Cheerful & friendly, he calls me 'my good man'.

Evening. In good light, my neighbour points out the two Severn bridges. The far shore & hills are near Weston-Super-Mare. My mind goes back to our time in Somerset, which feels like yesterday, not 20 years ago. Kay rings, full of praise for my *Selected Poems.* She suggests I write a poem for Elin, which I'd been thinking about.

31 July

A cloudy day for the last of the month. Quiet, reading, dozing. Small appetite: hospital meal times are wrong for me. Sandy rang and we talked about Les. In the interview, Colin's mention of me being in my eightieth year surprised me, as it should not have done. I have always felt younger, and I identify as a man who is nearly 80 with difficulty. How excited I was to get the job at Bath in 1988, when I thought I was too old, and to move to an area near to my original home, but new to me. I didn't expect to move again, and may not have done, if Les had lived.

1 August

Rain clouds. Gulls shrilling: for Lammas, Red King dead in the oakwoods, by accident or treachery. I would entertain M. with the story of Sir Walter Tyrrell, when, to disguise the direction of his flight, he reversed the shoes on his horse's hooves at the ford. Tyrrell's Ford, where I was attracted to a girl I met at a party in the hotel, and wrote a poem for her, when I was – how old? 16 or 17, perhaps. So, it goes back to the beginning of my life – desire, that draws the poem out of me.

From boyhood I had this feeling of being incomplete – until I was with Mieke. I feel now that we humans are incomplete beings: we contribute to the life of the generations. To fulfil is to hand on the life-process: to enable; to make possible. I think of this in drafting a poem about Archie, my great-grandson: How in welcoming a birth we may be more conscious of our own mortality. It may be a selfish thought, as I felt about Larkin's poem, 'Afternoons', in which he speaks of young mothers being pushed aside by their infants. This suggests to me a squib: babies in prams and buggies driving old codgers into the ditch (on Cemetery Road), pooping like so many Toads. Seriously, it calls to mind the purpose of life, whether it's more than what Chris's character Jack, in *Shifts*, calls 'the fucking biological imperative'. Are we only life-givers, feeding the generations? An old man may well ask. Ultimately it is a question of spirit, and the meaning of personal being.

2 August

Shower. Lie on my bed, writing /revising poems: 'Gulls', 'The Bridge' (2), 'What is poetry for?'. Reading *Powysland* & *The Magic Mountain*. Blanchard is good on Powys the man & thinker. He responds to him with essential humility, without defensiveness, as one 'peculiar' human to another. But he says nothing about Powys as a storyteller & creator of persons, where his genius as an 'artist' lies. How he saved me from a particular model or idea of 'manliness' encouraged by D.H. Lawrence!

We have to make friends of our weaknesses. Taking them too seriously, we go mad.

Revised 'Archie'.

I'm palpably lighter than when I was brought to The Heath, able to get in & out of bed without assistance, and walk short distances.

Afternoon. Initial attempt at poem for Elin. Re-reading *Flowering Earth* with a view to writing a homage to Donald Culross Peattie.

I can see what it was in his book that made it the only one I could read when Mieke died. It wasn't only his enthusiasm, but his gentle love for the first living things – protoplasm, plankton, sea weeds - the green world that gave life and sustains it. Somehow the bleakness of such vast ages containing so much death becomes, literally, a life-giving story.

5 August

At home now for two days. Mother's birthday. White buddleia in flower outside the front window. I shall probably have to go back into hospital soon to be fitted with a fistula.

7.

Poems

Nurses

1
She walks with beauty
carrying soiled bed sheets.
She is the lady with a torch
who comes silently in the night
soothing the disturbed,
watching, always watching,
where there is need.
She has a life outside
which she returns to,
but here too she is mother,
daughter, friend,
and the love an old man,
sleepless and afraid, dreams of.

2
This is for Jim, poet
of the ward, composing
in his head as he changes
a bed or brings cheer
with kindness, as once
to his father at the last.
For him, and for the many,
from Rhymney or Dowlais,
Tredegar or the Philippines.
Their gift is the art
of healing, which poetry
in its way, may hope to be.

The Bridge

The name speaks what it meant:
Wainsford – you can see
where the horses lumbered
and the laden wagons shook.
Here the stream gathers,
pools, seems to stand still
under the arch, before dashing on,
through shallows, into shadow.

A thing made for a purpose,
functional, economic,
not an object meant
to inspire a boy's first poem.

But nothing can stop the flow
when desire enters the world
and imagination, transfixed
by water under the stone arch,
senses in opaque depths
a source, a deeper mystery.

White Horse Hill

Who were they, masters
of the White Horse?

Bones from a barrow robbed
centuries ago will not answer,
pieces of pot are dumb,
their language is dust
that no one can translate.

Only listen.
          Put your ear
to the ground and feel it tremble,
sense the land
as it moves under you,
a rider borne on the back of the downs,
hair flying,
head pounding with blood.

Homage to the author of *Flowering Earth*

1
The brain, he said, is a spark
of dust in the universe.
But if a spark, desire
compels it to seek to know,
as he was drawn deep into time –
                    explorer
through age after age of being
and becoming, lover
of blue alga and the green leaf,
observer of bacteria and cell,
world-builders, makers
of the one stuff
that he knew in himself,
in the life he was part of.

2
Donald Culross Peattie:
plantsman, poet-naturalist.
What he knew he had by heart –
secrets visible in any flower –
                    one history
of billions of years,
the long adventure
through ages of sunlight
and dark, through ooze
and mud and mould,
and always everywhere
the elemental work
of water and sun and soils
composing the flowering earth.

3
How not love a man who spoke
of 'the peasantry of the grass'?

It was his feeling that moved me
when, grieving, I could bear
to read no other book but his.
What solace there? None
lest in the spirit that works
with and through death, quickening
both the mite and the mighty,
beings swarming in a drop of water,
diatom and leviathan, horsetail
in a ditch and kelp forest
in Pacific depths – all that is
always becoming, each self-being,
and the fact of love itself, as
we come awake to the thousand things.

Gulls

First, they were voices
speaking a language
familiar to me, but
untranslatable, that
sounded like *need need need*

I felt it was the sea
they were crying for,
the element that mothered them,
restless provider, giving
and withholding,
constantly unstill.

Ghost birds, pleading,
theirs was the voice
that troubled my cradle.
In age, it returns
with the night wind,
shrilling, bringing back
the beginning, promising the end.

Archie

Archie, great-
grandson, welcome
to a world that will be
for you, I pray, a place
to breathe in, free
of pestilence, and not
mired by human filth.

You will not know me,
Archie, unless in a poem
but may imagine me,
if you care to, thinking
of you, little boy in a bobble hat,
joy of your parents, delight
of all your kin.
    Soon, you will be ready
to set out, adventuring,
pushing aside old stories,
as you make your way
finding new words for a world
where, I trust, fresh winds will blow.

A squib for Archie

…'the fucking biological imperative'
   —Jack, in Christopher Meredith's *Shifts*

Beware, beware:
the codgers are on the run,
or would be, if they could run,
tottering,
throwing down sticks,
ejecting from wheelchairs,
falling off pavements into the ditch,
for here come the babies,
Poop Poop, a generation of Toads,
bouncing in buggies,
little folk, time lords
ferocious with innocence.
They mean no harm,
they intend no good;
they are hungry as sharks,
dangerous as road hogs
driven to drive.
So beware, oldies,
dads, grandpas, great
grandfathers.
Step aside, and instead
of falling, wave as they pass.

Lightning Source UK Ltd.
Milton Keynes UK
UKHW041500141021
392146UK00001B/26